SOCIO-LEGAL JOURNAL: VOLUME-V

SHIVANSH TIWARI

ISBN 978-1-63873-061-3

Contents

CHAPTER I

Article 3 and Its Ambiguity

Article 3 is made out of five particular components: torment, brutal, debasing, treatment and discipline. The previous three are unmistakable however related segments, alluding to the gravity of the Article 3 break and addressing a pecking order of the mischief endured by an individual. There is some trouble in determining where the 'section' edge for Article 3 is and where the distinctive variables for every one of the parts sit.

A finding of torment comprises the best seriousness and barbaric or corrupting moderately less so.The last two components allude to the kind of act/exclusion caused upon the person. Quite most demonstrations penetrating Article 3 concern 'treatment' however there are a few conditions that would all the more accurately be named as 'discipline'. A model is the place where an individual is more than once rebuffed and arraigned for a similar offense or discipline is self-assertive and unbalanced. For simplicity of conversation, this postulation alludes to 'treatment' as a conventional term for both treatment and discipline all through this section.

At the point when any Article 3 penetrate is asserted, the main rule to be met is that the treatment is of extraordinary enough seriousness to break Article 3.This is known as the de minimis ruleand will change contingent upon whether it is torment, cruel or debasing treatment that is being claimed. The rules are in reality less clear than one may from the start accept since there is no reasonable edge of seriousness that is all around material on the whole

Article 3 cases. The European Commission stressed this in the Greek Case when it held that each case must be settled on its own realities since what might be viewed as pitiless or unreasonable would shift among social orders and even inside various segments of them.

The subsequent point is that Article 3 comprises of both evenhanded and emotional parts. The likely utility of an emotional part, with regards to the current discussion is significant as it centers consideration around the casualty's understanding of the supposed break. By all appearances this permits more noteworthy extension for expanding the conditions where an Article 3 break may emerge.

The emotional component will be significant with regards to an assault case, for both assault complainants and litigants. The enduring caused to the individual may exclude actual harm yet can possibly cause extreme mental enduring over the span of lawful procedures. Anyway in corresponding to the milestone choice of the ECtHR that initially held that assault could add up to torment, the Court has gotten been more unequivocal and prohibitive in its standards for what can comprise

torment. Somewhat this will have a restricting impact upon any expansion of Article 3's ambis to remember obscurity for one or the other party for an assault case.

In finding out whether the essential limit has been met, the ECtHR in Ireland v UK, expressed that:

'[Any appraisal fair and square of severity] relies upon every one of the conditions of the case, like nature and setting of the treatment, its span, its physical or mental impacts and, in certain conditions, the sex, age, and condition of wellbeing of the person in question'.

The authority of Ireland corresponds with the abstract part of the Article 3 ambit and leaves further adaptability with regards to secrecy in assault cases with the end goal of individual contrasts.

One ought not fail to remember that an individual should likewise fulfill a target segment of Article 3 all together for a penetrate of that Article to be found. It is presented that the 'evenhanded' component is the demonstration or oversight, that, when thought about together, any imperative emotional component, can possibly add up to torment or barbaric or debasing treatment. Beneath the individual components of Article 3 are broke down momentarily thusly. The reason for doing so is twofold. It empowers the peruser to comprehend the limit's important to comprise a break of Article 3 and will give a perspective, against which an assault complainant's and litigant's Article 3 rights, comparable to the namelessness banter, can be talked about.

CHAPTER II

Crime Prevention: What can the Government do to Lower the Crime Rates

To diminish wrongdoing and renew networks, it is important to build up a procedure that can successfully mediate in the pattern of brutality before it claims the future. An essential focal point of our endeavours, along these lines, ought to be to reach and guide our Nation's young people who now, by the age of 18, stand up to additional significant good choices than their folks' generation looked in a whole lifetime. A model of compelling youth intercession exists. There are many people all through the country who have the demonstrated ability to supportive of vide the direction and model that have the force to divert in danger adolescents to beneficial and positive exercises. The significance and novel force of these committed local area pioneers can be appreciated best considering the extent of the issues experienced by the present young people and the terrible history of numerous regular, expertly planned programs for in danger youths. All through the Nation, violations submitted by adolescents, who frequently express an unpleasant feeling of impassion, have made a public discernment that a segment of the forthcoming age is now lost—past help. Reports and measurable examinations likewise uncover that the plague of otherworldly discomfort furthermore, brutality is anything but a confined "downtown" issue furthermore, that it is influencing groups of each pay level.

All through the Nation, young people from rural neighborhoods and provincial networks, as internal city adolescents, are squandering, losing, and taking their lives. 5,000 kids kick the bucket every year as a aftereffect of attacks, ailment, or suicide.It is anticipated that 1 out of 7 young people who are currently between the ages of 10 and 18 will flee from home. Every year, 1.5 million youngsters are living on the streets.

A significant number of these kids go to the medication exchange or prostitution as a wellspring of cash. Patterns in social decisions among youths demonstrate that the emergency will deteriorate if viable mediation and backing are not given. In a ongoing overview of eighth graders, 33% of the respondents said they utilize illegal medications and 15 percent said they had smashed in excess of five jazzed up beverages in succession in the previous 2 weeks.In 1996, the best expansion in birth to young people was to young ladies more youthful than 15 years of age. The guns homicide rate among 10-through 14-year-olds more than multiplied somewhere in the range of 1985 and 1992, and self destruction rates for these young people expanded by 120% from 1980 to 1992.5 Obviously, our Nation's customary reactions to the issues of youth savagery have not been viable notwithstanding the large numbers of dollars that have been put resources into them. Analysts project that adolescent captures for savage wrongdoing will dramatically increase by 2010. A new cross country review announced that posse participation in the United States has developed to additional than 650,000 adolescents who are associated with 25,000 groups. Accordingly, a monstrous crackdown was dispatched by the FBI, which made 133 teams that brought about 92,000 captures and 35,000 convictions cross country all through a 4-year period.However in numerous cases, these captures did close to move a "bubble" of wrongdoing to another area. In the words of one prison guard in a State where a big part of a 38,000-man jail populace has been recognized as gangsters, "The issue doesn't disappear. At the point when the local area disposes of its pack issue, that issue is then moved to the restorative establishment. Indeed, it turns out to be more intensified."Until this point in time, most assets and endeavors to save our Country's youngsters have been focused to downtown populaces. Youngsters in low-pay neighborhoods have felt the most serious effect of the good free-fall that is besetting the cutting edge because their networks do not have the monetary dependability In fields including posse action, unwed youngster

nurturing, and substance misuse, a considerable lot of the most powerful problem solvers are people who have by and by experienced and beat the issues they urge others to survive. Their day by day lives give a reasonable illustration of the qualities and norms they advance, and their faithful, long haul obligation to the youngsters they serve has won the certainty, trust, and regard of adolescents, even the individuals who had been considered incorrigible by the social help situation. Disregarding their viability, by and large guidelines have supportive of prohibited such grassroots volunteers from giving administrations in their neighborhoods since they need scholastic degrees or expert confirmation. "Saving" a youngster from their climate may not be the arrangement. The salvage method of traditional projects overlooks the worth producing, intervening constructions that exist inside the young people's own networks (families, neighborhood affiliations, and so forth) and may, indeed, sabotage and usurp them. It is expected to be that the arrangement lies in the value of the individuals who are outside the local area. This is genuine even of the much-commended guide favorable to grams, which every now and again sidestep guardians and neighbors. What message does a youngster get through programs that are based with the understanding that good examples should be brought into their homes what's more, networks? The existences of youngsters cannot be rescued through external intercession that overlooks the need of supporting and fortifying their networks. The way to setting up consistent and practical help lies in utilizing the native, "regular antibodies" of a local area, which have the ability to avoid cultural sickness. Focusing on just a single region of a complex of interrelated issues may not work.

Conversely, individual area based effort addresses the entire individual and the interrelated factors that influence an individual's life. For instance, one of the best substance misuse programs I have experienced, the San Antonio-based Victory Cooperation, doesn't zero in only on eradicating medication and liquor fixation yet additionally consolidates projects to rejoin and fortify families, meet the necessities of the offspring of addicts, and give instructive and work openings.Through Victory Fellowship's great Christian rendition of the Boy Scouts, the Royal Rangers, youngsters who have effectively defeated their addictions work as good examples for young men age also, more seasoned, managing them in undertakings of local area administration and community duty.As of late, a coordinated effort of grassroots activities in Washington called Hands Across DC has made a model far reaching system. Five gatherings have united to 'dive deep' into pained neighborhoods, supporting the overcomers of manslaughter victims, preparing detained men to satisfy their duties to their families and networks, furthermore, giving profitable exercises and instructive openings for youngsters. Native, grassroots, youth intercession supportive of grams all through the Nation have shown us that answers for this emergency exist. Neighborhood-based methodologies have been strikingly powerful in eliminating as opposed to just dislodging youth viciousness. Records of their endeavors show us, notwithstanding, that there is no alternate way to inciting the change in youngsters' vision and qualities. Such inside changes are the reap of long haul consistent exertion, nonstop accessibility, and the individual illustration of grown-ups who have submitted themselves to a calling to rescue youthful lives.

CHAPTER III

A Deeper Look Into The History of Death Penalty

In written history, Capital Punishment was introduced in the British Colonial law under Indian Panel Code (IPC) 1860. The law covered close to two-third of India and was not enforceable or acknowledged by regal states and bigger autonomous states like Jammu and Kashmir, Baroda (Vadodara), and Hyderabad to make reference to a rare sorts of people who followed their own strategies for Capital Punishment. Furthermore, the Colonial rulers perceived customary and strict laws predominant around then in the country, which were at fluctuation with the Judo-Christian Laws of Capital Punishment. For instance, in an upper east locale, the Scheduled Tribes followed and kept on after their deep rooted techniques for discipline and are managed frequently without going to courts. In Independent India absent a lot of consultation, Indian Panel Code propounded by British Colonial rulers got appropriate to all residents of free India.

The decisions of the Supreme Court of India and various enactments authorized by the Parliament of India after freedom all things considered brings up that the judgment and enactment had certain way of thinking that Death Penalty ought to be forced uniquely in 'the most extraordinary of uncommon cases'. Be that as it may, capital punishment as a response to coldhearted social acts of 'Sati' was authorized and considered as wrongdoing culpable with death under The Commission of Sati (Prevention) Act, 1987. Essentially, required capital punishment has been endorsed for second time guilty parties of enormous scope opiates dealing. It ought to be referenced that opiates dealing has been widespread on most worldwide lines of the country. Comparative discipline has been endorsed under the Punishment of Atrocity Act 1989 against the monstrosities of Scheduled Casts and Scheduled Tribes.

The conflict of the prior brief investigation is that Capital Punishment is in the antiquated civilisation of India and contemporary vote based India keeps on being uncertain issue of discussion, conversation and thought on good, social and worth premises exuding out of Sanatan Dharma, Jainism and Buddhism. Indeed, even Islamic laws forced by Mughal Emperors invited conversation notwithstanding clear Islamic decision on the issue of Capital Punishment. It was additionally compounded by the pilgrim rulers by forcing technique for equity straightforwardly drawn from the at that point existing of British Laws. Thus, it is creator's dispute that the entire issue of Capital Punishment requires further examination, thought and reflection before the equivalent could be along the side chosen by anybody concerned. In old India, much before Christian time, Kautilya recommended capital punishment for verity of wrongdoings utilizing various techniques for doing capital punishment inside Sanatan Dharma (L.N. Rangarajan, Kautilya: The Arthshastra, Penguin: 1985, pp. 494–495). In the resulting hundreds of years, there have been incredible arrangements of discussions and conversations on the issue of capital punishment. At that point Mughal Empire presented Islamic standards and Islamic strategy for equity for capital punishment. It was stylish from the fourteenth century forward followed by establishments and compounded by the burden of outsider Judo-Christian or European technique for equity got by British pilgrim rulers identified with capital punishment.

The current strategy for regulating equity radiates out of these chronicled occasions and as counter response of nearby and local customs of equity. The central purpose of the contention is that India has had numerous standards of administration, meaning of 'off-base' and 'right', wrongdoing and discipline and assortment of techniques for directing equity including capital punishment. Subsequently, there is need to rethink the issue of capital punishment inside the adaptable multi-strict, multi-lingual and multiregional viewpoint predominant practices in each etymological district and geographic area. It would require opening up of more extensive degree for impartial equity to all.

CHAPTER IV

Human Right and Police: A Bird's Eye View

Abstract

The acknowledgment of common liberties relies upon numerous elements. Among the different things, the job of Justice Administration authorities of the state (particularly Police) assume essential part. In any country, police have tremendous forces in the execution of Law and Order. Alongside powers and capacities, they have various obligations, responsible to state, and public at huge through their demonstrations. Common liberties insurance and their acknowledgment also rely upon the personal conduct standard of the police. As a law authorizing organization their demeanor, moral, moral direct is vital in the advancement of Human Rights. Being a crucial office between the state and public, this paper is an unobtrusive endeavor to feature the forces of the police in the assurance and advancement of basic freedoms.

Introduction

The fundamental point of law is to build up a contention free society and to prepare the men to live in harmony furthermore, amicability to lead an existence effortlessly. This thus will assist every general public with setting up the principles of social equity on equivalent balance and ready to assist the men with understanding their normal or common liberties ensured both globally and public domains. To set up a contention free society, in an administration, the law authorizing offices, particularly the establishment of Police assume an indispensable part in the execution of the lawfulness dicta as imagined either by the Constitution, Executive, Legislature or Judiciary. In any case, unnecessary utilization of forces gave on them, or in misinterpretation of any law would equivalent to the infringement of common liberties and forestalls the free exercise of the rights public on the loose

Concept of Human Rights

Basic liberties being basic normal rights, they are perceived globally through a number of legitimate instruments. The fundamental way of thinking of common liberties to start with is to ensure the natural poise of human people and to advance their life and freedom to do equity with no abnormality from the standards of law. Notwithstanding, in the later many years, particularly in the last part of the sixties and mid seventies the basic legacy of humankind tenet has broadened the domain of jurisprudential vistas of basic liberties to cover that of the States and other legitimate substances. Taking into account the expansionist philosophical precepts of basic freedoms, basic liberties may be depicted as Human Rights for all and All for Human Rights. This meaning of human rights covers all people, which incorporate the lawful people. Globally states creatures subjects of global law and went into different arrangements to convey their commitments in civil law, they go about as defenders of basic liberties of their populace and all people

Powers of Police

In any general public the fundamental article and point of law is to ease the power of contentions and set up the men for the reformist advancement of a general public. Subsequently, the execution of the lawful dicta, the state regularly engages the police to authorize the lawfulness to set up harmony and security. This thusly implies, the law upholding officials particularly police, have colossal forces and also obligations. As officials of the states, police need to implement their rights to forestall wrongdoing in the general public. This being the primary assignment of police, the law of a state engages police lawfully to authorize measures, strategies, and means, to forestall criminal offenses or to recognize and catch the culprits of those offenses. The different law authorizing organizations of police are enabled with countless forces. They are by and large, notice, requesting, recognizable proof, examination, summons, capture, detainment, development of limitation in a specific zone or working according to the request for the legal executive, assaults on private spots of people, search and seizure, assortment of proof, debacle the board obligations, knowledge and security, traffic obligations, insurance of more fragile areas, digital wrongdoings, drug dealing support of records, implementation of social enactment, utilizing logical and different strategies to extricate proof and so forth.

Human Rights and Police

International Scenario

To secure and advance the common liberties of the people across the globe, the United Countries received various records to manage the states in the requirement of lawful system at the public level. Among the different records that manage basic liberties, the accompanying have an immediate bearing on the working and exercise of rights by the police in the requirement of common freedoms. They are as a rule: The Universal Declaration of Human Rights, the Covenant on Economics, Social and Cultural rights, the Covenant on Civil and Political Rights, and other global records. The records that uniquely worry with the police are :

Declaration on the Protection of All Persons from being Subjected to Torture and other

Cruel, Inhuman or Degrading Treatment or Punishment (1975)

UN Code of Conduct for Law Enforcement Officials (1979)

UN Principles on the Effective Prevention and Investigation of Extra-Legal, Arbitrary and

Summary Executions (1989)

UN Declaration on the Protection of All Persons from Enforced Disappearances (1992)

UN Convention against Torture and Other Cruel, Inhuman or Degrading Treatment or

Punishment (1984)

UN International Covenant on Civil and Political Rights (ICCPR), (1966)

UN Basic Principles on the Use of Force and Firearms by Law Enforcement Officials

(1990)

UN Standard Minimum Rules for the Treatment of Prisoners (1977)

UN Body of Principles for the Protection of All Persons under Any Form of Detention or

Imprisonment (hereafter referred to as Body of Principles) (1988)

UN Convention on the Rights of the Child (1989)

UN Rules for the Protection of Juveniles Deprived of their Liberty (1990)

UN Declaration on the Elimination of all forms of discrimination against Women (1967)

UN Declaration of Basic Principles of Justice for Victims of Crime and Abuse of Powers

(1990)

Apart from the above, the office of the UN High Commissioner for Human Rights adopted a

number of practical guides highlighting the linkage that exist between police and human

rights.

National Regime

The constitution of India is the principal National archive straightforwardly embraces the points and articles of the Charter of the United Nations and the UDHR. The composers of the Constitution roused by the Ideals of Human Rights, without precedent for the records of Human Rights, bifurcated the combination of justiciable (Civil and Political Rights), and non-justiciable (Economic, Social and Social Rights), embraced them as Fundamental Rights and Directive Principles of State Strategy. Among the different arrangements, Art. 22 of the Constitution explicitly specifies that any people captured should be educated regarding the grounds promptly and be created before the judge with in 24 hours or at the most punctual. Aside from the article, various decisions conveyed by the Supreme Court of India, broadly deciphering different arrangements of the constitution, particularly Article 21 of the constitution and set out various protections for the implementation of criminal equity framework with no abuse by police. In a number cases, the court held that at whatever point, the privileges of the residents are attacked with a devilish or malignant goal, which incorporate the unreasonable utilization of force by police, the court can practice the ward, to repay the casualty by granting suitable remuneration and indicate any other healing system. In such manner, the Judiciary has developed the Public Interest Prosecution or Social Action Litigation and discarded various cases, particularly to maintain the common liberties of public everywhere from the hostile and noxious demonstrations of police.

Conclusion

Police assume a fundamental part in the requirement of peace and lawfulness. The achievement of criminal equity frameworks basically relies upon the appropriate working of law implementing authorities, particularly the police. Simultaneously, as dependable officials of the express, the police have a burdensome errand to secure and advance common freedoms as an integral part of the state. The prescribed procedures received by police, particularly considering all segments of public which incorporates denounced and casualties have rights and they should be increased to the most extreme degree with no deviation while releasing their forces and capacities. From the reception of Police Act 1861, until date various laws and guidelines received by both the Union and States to direct the personal conduct standards of police in the advancement of basic liberties. Yet, as appropriately brought up by the Police Commission and the Model Police Manual the unnecessary utilization of power or force should be directed to forestall the corrupt demonstrations of the police. Simultaneously, the political pioneers, pseudo fundamentalists on different checks need to quit abusing police to sub serve their personal stakes. This sort of shady strategies are embraced by numerous multiple times particularly to settle the common debates too at times where police have no job past the restrictions of law endorsed therein1

What are the Implications of the War on Terror on the Enforcement of Criminal Law: A Case Study of US

Introduction

Since the 9/11 fear based oppressor assaults, the requirement for expanded counterterrorism (CT) endeavors at the government and state levels has taken the spotlight in open security endeavors. In any case, similarly significant is the exertion at the nearby law implementation organization (LEA) level. A report by the U.S. Office of State clarified that The proceeded with danger of illegal intimidation has pushed homegrown arranged ness commitments to the actual top of the law authorization plan. . . . [T]his limit should be considered as much a staple of law requirement tasks as wrongdoing examination, criminal insight, also, wrongdoing counteraction." (U.S. Division of State, 2005) Illegal intimidation has become a nearby local area concern, and LEAs have expanded the degree of assets dedicated to CT endeavors. The International Association of Chiefs of Police portrays a critical requirement for law implementation's consideration regarding CT endeavors, expressing "nearby police initiative is direly required . . . [to] mollify feelings and concerns [of] resident view of risk" of psychological militant danger (International Association of Heads of Police, 2003, p. 5). Today, CT is a significant piece of numerous neighborhood LEAs'plans ,particularly those in metropolitan regions or potentially in high-hazard wards.

In any case LEAs are as yet creating extensive CT procedures and surveying what bearing these plans should take. Fusing CT exercises into a division is a critical hierarchical change measure. Based This record is an examination report submitted to the U.S. Branch of Justice. This report has not been distributed by the Department. Conclusions or perspectives communicated are those of the author(s) also, don't really mirror the authority position or strategies of the U.S. Branch of Justice. Effects of Law Enforcement's Focus on Counterterrorism/Homeland Securityon the report Protecting Your Community from Terrorism, which out- lines how a nearby police division can get ready and execute home- land security (HS) plans, "even those [agencies] that vibe sure oftheir charges should roll out huge improvements to their design, strategies, systems, faculty skill, preparing, and spending plans—all with as it were their own rules or guidelines to guarantee achievement" (Police Executive Examination Forum, 2003). A few pundits have contended that, albeit the United States is taking huge steps in CT work, "the make-up of Washington's post-9/11 homegrown insight engineering keeps on reflecting a government driven direction" (Chalk and Rosenau, 2004, p. 19). A normal analysis is that government organizations, like the FBI, are hesitant to impart knowledge to nearby regions. At first, government intelligence organizations were to some degree distrustful of illegal intimidation related information provided by state and neighborhood LEAs (Chalk and Rosenau, 2004; Jen-families, 2008; Progressive Policy Institute, 2003). Regardless of the insight by pundits that the insight local area may dismiss data from state and neighborhood LEAs, the FBI has perceived that accomplishment against psychological warfare is best accomplished through participation among different government, state, and neighborhood law implementation wellbeing organizations (Caruso, 2002). Others contend that LEAs fill in as the establishment for successfully evaluating dangerening exercises inside their networks, in manners better than the FBI can (Bodrero, 1999). The effect of such centering occasions as 9/11 might be better surveyed after a huge time has passed (McGarrell, Freilich, what's more, Chermak, 2007). The motivation behind this investigation is to analyze the present status of CT what's more, HS in LEAs nine years following the 9/11 fear monger assaults and the long haul changes that huge metropolitan police offices have made to oblige this new job. In the remainder of this foundation area, we sum up a portion of the central points of contention encompassing CT endeavors at the LEA level.

Objectives

The issues raised above give the setting where this report is grounded, the motivation behind which is to give some experimental setting for seeing what the fear monger danger has meant for neighborhood policing associations, especially those in huge metropolitan regions, while likewise con- sidering the adjustments regarding their expenses and advantages to public wellbeing arrangement. Specifically, with subsidizing from the National Institute of Justice (NIJ), this examination tends to the accompanying exploration questions:

• How has law implementation's systems advanced to meet leavements' drawn out CT and HS prerequisites? What long haul authoritative changes were made? How much has this center made new operational requests? What impact has the core interest on CT and HS had on preparing and official abilities sets required?

• How has law requirement resourced its CT and HS exercises? How has government subsidizing for these exercises advanced and what are the ramifications for LEAs?

This record is an exploration report submitted to the U.S. Branch of Justice. This report has notbeen distributed by the Department. Assessments or perspectives communicated are those of the author(s) also, don't really mirror the authority position or approaches of the U.S. Branch of Justice. Effects of Law Enforcement's Focus on Counterterrorism/Homeland Security

• What benefits and difficulties are related with this new zero in on CT and HS?

• What has been the advancement of combination focuses? What key patterns are related with LEAs' present way to deal with CT, including data sharing, utilizing innovation, and coordination exercises?

• What are the current advantages related with this drawn out concentration on CT and HS? What scientific framework can be used to assess the potential costs?

Approach

Case Study Approach

The RAND group, in conference with NIJ project staff, recognized the accompanying determination measures: (1) LEAs situated in major metropolitan zones and juris- styles with a high danger of fear monger assaults, (2) LEAs from various areas of the nation, and (3) LEAs that changed they would say with CT and HS. The five enormous metropolitan LEAs were chosen as a result of their initiative around there and the moderately undeniable degree of psychological oppression hazard that their purviews face. Two of the divisions are situated in Level I metropolitan territories (viewed as at the most noteworthy danger for psychological oppression), furthermore, the other three divisions are situated in Tier II metropolitan territories (next most noteworthy danger for illegal intimidationThe Boston, Houston, Las Vegas Metropolitan, and Miami-Dade LEAs are among the 50 biggest police divisions in the United States;the Los Angeles County Sheriff's Department is the biggest sheriff's division in the United States (Reaves, 2007). We chose the Las Vegas Metropolitan PD in light of the potential psychological oppressor danger the city faces given its notorious status. Houston, Miami-Dade, and the Boston PDs are situated in significant port urban communities. The Houston PD's new experience with two significant typhoons in 2005 likewise assisted with testing a number of the division's reaction abilities and its general readiness. The Miami-Dade PD's locale addresses a significant section point into the United States for the Caribbean and encompassing zones. The Boston PD was chosen in light of the immediate effect that 9/11 had on this metropolitan region, pushing this office in the cutting edge of law requirement's new job in CT and HS. The entirety of the divisions have significant worldwide air terminals. At long last, the Los Angeles County Sheriff's Office was chosen since it addresses the biggest sheriff's office in the United States and is mindful, alongside the Orange County Sheriff's Department, for Region One Homeland Security in California. Additionally, it was chosen in light of the fact that, in California, sheriff's specialties are answerable for law authorization shared guide at the neighborhood and territorial levels. This office additionally has a long history of tending to fear Attributes of Case Sudy Law Enforcement Agencies LEA Geographic RegionLevel of Metropolitan Area Size (No. of Full-Time Sworn Personnel)a Oversees District's Combination Center

Boston PD Northeast Tier II 1,961 Yes Houston PD Southwest Tier I 5,092 Yes Las Vegas Metropolitan PD West Tier II 2,674 No Los Angeles County Sheriff's Department West Tier I 8,239 Yes Miami-Dade PD Southeast Tier II 3,094 No The quantity of full-time sworn faculty is as of September 2004 and comes from Reaves (2007). This record is an exploration report submitted to the U.S. Branch of Justice. This report has not been distributed by the Department. Assessments or perspectives communicated are those of the author(s) also, don't really mirror the authority position or arrangements of the U.S. Division of Justice. Effects of Law Enforcement's Focus on Counterterrorism/Homeland Security dangers and creating data sharing constructions even before the 9/11 fear monger assaults.

CHAPTER VI

The Insanity Defense: A Loophole for Criminals

Introduction

The present article reviews research on the insanity defence in the 5-year period spanning 1993 to 1997. Publications used in this review were obtained through a search of Psychinfo and MedLine.

Demographic Characteristics of Insanity Acquittees

A lot of examination has been committed to inspecting the segment qualities of craziness acquittees furthermore, generally, these considers paint a genuinely reliable representation. Maybe the biggest single investigation of not blameworthy by reason of craziness (NGRI) acquittees was directed in the United States and included information from eight states (Cirincione et al., 1995).

Gender

Despite the fact that sexual orientation is regularly included as a variable in research on the madness guard, not many examinations have set out to completely come close male and female madness acquittees. As far as anyone is concerned, the lone exhaustive examination of male and female madness acquittees in the previous 5 years was led by Seig, Ball, and Menninger (1995) in the province of Colorado. Their examination uncovered critical contrasts as far as mental and criminal history just as segment factors.

Criminal History and Current Offense

Examination exploring the criminal history of respondents who argue craziness by and large, 75% of respondents have had earlier captures (Sprout and Williams, 1994; Cirincione et al., 1995). Over the span of our audit, we noticed that reviews shifted between refering to earlier feelings or refering to earlier captures as a proportion of preacquittal contact with the law. As anyone might expect, those contemplates that utilized earlier feelings as a proportion of earlier contact with the crook equity framework yielded a lot of lower rates (e.g., 37%; Hodgins, 1993). Notwithstanding prevalent thinking that the common madness acquittee has been charged with murder, research has exhibited that solitary a minority has really dedicated murder or even endeavored murder.

General Demographics Outside North America

Examination from Europe has yielded marginally unexpected outcomes in comparison to that led in the United States and Canada. Gibbons et al. (1997) led a retrospective investigation portraying all madness acquittees in Ireland between a long time 1850 and 1995. Their appraisal demonstrated that the craziness guard is more comprehensively utilized in North America than in Ireland, where it gives off an impression of being saved for just the most genuine cases (95% of acquittees had been charged with fierce offenses, 72% of which were manslaughter or child murder). The proportion of guys to females likewise gave off an impression of being to some degree lower in Ireland, with a more noteworthy extent of madness acquittees being female (5:1 when contrasted with the10:1 proportion found in North America).

Assessment Issues

Broad analysis coordinated toward legal experts just as the conceivably extreme outcomes of being seen not as blameworthy by reason of madness seem to have been main thrusts behind ongoing examination on the craziness protection. In the previous 5 years, countless investigations have been directed to inspect all the more intently the clinical appraisal of the individuals who argue madness. Exploration has tended to the issue from various points, zeroing in on the facilitiesties in which pretrial assessments are completed, the capabilities of those who perform measurable appraisals, the instruments that are or ought to be used in this cycle, and new systems to help in choices about contingent discharge, just as strategies for assessing and better anticipating result of contingent delivery.

Specific Populations

Examination on criminal duty has likewise reached out past the severe limits of the overall mental writing, with analysts endeavoring to recognize mind dysfunctions related with criminal conduct. In particular, Raine et al. (1994) estimated mind working using positron emanation tomography (PET) inside a gathering of craziness respondents who had submitted murder and a gathering of coordinated controls. Results demonstrated that killers who are arguing craziness are portrayed by a particular prefrontal brokenness

Factors Affecting Verdicts of Insanity

Mark Jury Research

Research with mock juries illustrates that hearers embrace a far reaching and cautious thought of an enormous number of pertinent variables prior to delivering a decision. Among the components refered to as significant are presence of a crazy issue (e.g., Lymburner, 1997), master observer declaration (Rogers, Bagby, and Perera, 1993; Whittemore and Ogloff, 1995), police proof (Rogers et al., 1993), the litigant's thought process (e.g., Finkel and Groscup, 1997), and how much the file offense was arranged (e.g., Boardman, Stafford, and Ben-Porath, 1996; Lymburner, 1997).

Archival Research

Exploration has commonly shown that females are bound to be absolved than are guys and that respondents under the age of 20 are more averse to effectively raise the madness guard than more established respondents (Cirincione et al., 1995). In Japan, Satsumi and Oda (1995) found that inside a populace of madness evaluatees determined to have significant psychoses, those who were discovered not mindful were bound to be hitched and living with others in their own homes than the individuals who were discovered dependable or of lessened duty.

Detention and Release Patterns for Insanity Acquittees

Writing here shows that there is pretty much nothing consistency across purviews as for the time span for which madness acquittees are confined. For instance, in Quebec, Hodgins (1993) found that the normal length of hospitalization for madness acquittees was very nearly 7 a long time with a warrant locally for an extra 15 months. Interestingly, research led in California demonstrated that the mean length of hospitalization for madness acquittees was 2.8 years (Marques, Haynes, and Nelson, 1993).

Recidivism

Examination on recidivism rates has discovered that, generally speaking, rearrest rates during restrictive delivery went from 2% to 16%, with these numbers expanding considerably for longer-term follow-up periods (i.e., 42–56%). In Quebec, Hodgins (1993) directed a subsequent investigation of all people who had been found NGRI or unsuitable to stand preliminary in Quebec from 1973 through 1975. Seven years postrelease, 37.8% of those alive and living in Canada had been indicted for another criminal offense, however practically all recidivism had happened in the first 3 years after release. In the 7 years following release, 61% of these patients were rehospitalized. In Heilbrun and Griffin's (1993) survey of the local area- based criminological treatment of madness acquittees, they found that none of their example had carried out a vicious wrongdoing during the 1.5-year follow-up enough said. In Oregon just 5% were captured while on restrictive delivery, however another investigation directed in this state demonstrated a rearrest pace of 42% after acquittees were delivered from the survey board purview (Heilbrun and Griffin, 1993).

Impact of Changes to Insanity Defence

Conversely, Cirincione (1996) found that, while changes zeroing in being investigated techniques were probably not going to prompt authoritative changes, changes at the demeanor stage were bound to prompt discernible changes (Cirincione, 1996). In particular, such changes will in general build the quantity of craziness requests that are settled through supplication dealing, which in itself is firmly identified with a liable decision. Steady with Cirincione's (1996) decision that changes at the attitude stage lead to discernible changes, ongoing revisions to Canada's Criminal Code (i.e., Bill C-30) seem to have had a huge effect. Bill C-30 changed the decision of not blameworthy by reason of madness to not criminally mindful by reason of mental problem.

Rights of Defendants

As we have seen, the choice to raise a madness safeguard conveys genuine results for respondents, which may incorporate lengthier confinements than would be forced upon people indicted for comparable offenses. Nonetheless, regardless of the possibly genuine results of arguing craziness, a conventional assessment of the respondents' competency to raise a craziness safeguard is frequently not led, nor are competency to stand preliminary appraisals regularly completed for the individuals who argue craziness. While some have contended that the lawful cycle guarantees that a litigant should essentially be able to raise the craziness safeguard, late exploration seems to question this statement. Indeed, contemplates recommend that by far most of respondents are both badly educated about the madness safeguard just as inept to settle on a choice at the hour of the preliminary.

Conclusion

While an impressive, and maybe lopsided, measure of psycholegal research has zeroed in on the madness protection, it has all the earmarks of being the situation that not one or the other this examination nor the numerous adjustments in law and strategy that have been made throughout the years have fulfilled the public's interests about the craziness protection. These worries, nonetheless, seem, by all accounts, to be founded on various confusions. Experimental exploration has reliably exhibited that the madness protection is seldom utilized, is by and large just effective for the most seriously disarranged respondents, what's more, that madness acquittees are frequently confined for expanded periods. Accordingly, doubtlessly our consideration need not be coordinated toward further exact examination around there, but instead toward spreading our current condition of information.

CHAPTER VII

Rape Anonymity: The Arguments Examined

Complaint Anonymity

Assault is an especially egregious wrongdoing and the shame appended to public information on being an assault casualty deters ladies from detailing the offense and conviction rates are low. The contention of 'causing ladies to feel more ready to report the wrongdoing' has frequently been refered to during parliamentary discussion by those for assault complainant namelessness. Ongoing MoJ measurements likewise show that the quantity of assaults recorded has expanded essentially during the most recent decade, an ascent that some will ascribe straightforwardly to complainant namelessness. However prominently there has been no relating ascend in conviction rates. Proof shows that conviction rates for assault have fallen altogether, from a conviction pace of 33% in 1977. They currently remain astoundingly low notwithstanding an increment in assault charges year on year. In 2009 conviction rates for assault were discovered to be the most minimal in Europe,or to underline the gravity of this measurement, lower part of 33 states. Conviction rates remained at 5.6% in England and Wales and 2.9% in Scotland, though by correlation France had a conviction pace of 25%.

These figures propose that the contentions for complainant namelessness are impressively more perplexing than basically 'reassuring assault complainants to report the wrongdoing'. Contentions preferring assault complainant obscurity is really founded on various interrelated components, with recorded roots, yet which keep on oppressing assault complainants and ladies all the more by and large today. Apparently, the most harming of these variables is the presence of 'assault legends'. Assault legends are broadly held cultural assumptions regarding what is viewed as proper conduct for ladies, what sort of lady is fit for being a genuine assault casualty and in what conditions the assault ought to happen to be classed as assault. Temkin notes:

'[T]here is most likely no other criminal offense that is unpredictably identified with more extensive social perspectives and assessment of the casualty's lead as rape. When defied with a record of a supposed assault, people will in general react to it against the setting of their own convictions and understandings about sex connections by and large, suitable conduct for people, and the standards and customs of consensual associations'.

In view of this contentions are gathered for assault complainant secrecy into two gatherings. The first spotlights on the chronicled improvements that have occurred and affected sex relations, while the second spotlights on the assault legends.

Rape as Violence and Male Power

As per Brownmiller, the human species have built up a complex mental framework organized around the experience of pleasure.A man can possibly excite the sexual interest of a lady whenever since his 'mental (sexual) encourage' isn't subject to her physiological preparation to mate. Brownmiller encourages that '[W]hat everything reduces to is that the human male can assault'. At the point when a man understood his own capacity to assault, his penis was set up as an intense weapon of power against women.Additionally another force relationship, characterized by sexuality was set up between the genders, where the male was prevailing sex.

Assault and sexual brutality have subsequently built up sex imbalance all the more by and large. Assault is 'supported' in social orders where the force battle between the genders stays pervasive. Natural contrasts, exemplified by man's boss size and strength have just intensified the impact. To shield themselves from a man's weapon of assault, ladies have been compelled to submit to a male relative for assurance and to monitor her celibacy. A second result of men's prevailing position is that male centric overall sets of laws have arisen. Laws were planned by men in light of a legitimate concern for men: the early law of assault being one model. Assault of a lady was viewed as an infringement of her virtue and monogamy and an offense against the domain of the man whose charge she was under. Today, the UK's overall set of laws has advanced past numerous old laws, yet it is no less man centric or oppressive towards ladies. Kennedy fights that the discussion encompassing namelessness for assault respondents is one obvious illustration of ladies' current legitimate disparity.

Rape Myths

The impacts of assault legends are multi-overlap. Society derides most of assault casualties who don't adjust to a given legend, deteriorating and reprimanding them for what has occurred. The casualty's conduct previously, during, and after the attack is investigated to assess her duty. A 2005 report arranged for Amnesty International found that 29% individuals asked said ladies who neglected to say no, were in any event incompletely liable for being assaulted, while 8% considered the casualty absolutely mindful, 28% accepted that a lady who acted in a coquettish way was mostly liable for being assaulted and 6% absolutely capable, 26% accepted that a lady who was smashed was at any rate halfway liable for being assaulted and 4% considered her absolutely dependable. The result of cultural bias is that it debilitate assault casualties from revealing wrongdoing: it influences the casualty's experience of and treatment all through the legal interaction and antagonistically influences the odds of a (blameworthy) litigant being effectively sentenced in court. It can likewise be connected to the excessively high steady loss rates in assault cases, the outcome of which is that just about 6% of announced assaults will get a conviction in court.

Assault fantasies are compounded by 'social contents': mental portrayals that permit people to clarify certain results through sensible groupings of occasions. This incorporates the conviction that if a lady dresses with a particular goal in mind, or shows certain types of conduct then she is probably going to get assaulted, as opposed to tolerating that an individual person is able to do such a wrongdoing.

The Real Rape Scenario

The primary assault legend concerns the situation needed for an assault to be considered 'genuine'. It includes an assault by a vicious more peculiar, in a dim road, late around evening time, where a virtuous woman battles to guard herself. She gets substantially injury and reports the offense to the police quickly a short time later. This is the common situation envisioned when individuals consider assault assaults and any deviation acts against the person in question. Examination has proposed that the probability of an assault respondent being accused of the wrongdoing of assault expanded with the degree to which an assault casualty and assault adjusted to this cliché ideal.The singular parts of this situation all demonstration antagonistically on the choice of a casualty to report the wrongdoing, or for a revealed wrongdoing to end in a conviction.

The situational setting of this first assault fantasy is at chances with the more normal setting for an assault: some place private like the home. The respondent is probably going to be somebody known to the person in question, a spouse, beau, work associate or ex-accomplice. Anyway it is assessed that in around 80% of assault cases the litigant is known to the complainant. Shockingly the nearer the connection between the litigant and casualty, the more uncertain a conviction is to occur.In court the commonality of a relationship is viewed as a moderating situation, making the offense less genuine.

Equality with Rape Complainants

A second argument in favour of defendant anonymity in rape cases is one of equality before the law. The law should be 'tit for tat', and rape complainants and defendants should receive equal treatment in the legal process. Anonymity provisions for one party should be matched by anonymity provisions for the other. This argument has been put forward on a number of occasions during parliamentary debates, including when Mr Burley said '[I]f we are singling out this particular area of the criminal justice system for special treatment, why should it not apply equally to both men and women?'

Televised research involving mock jury deliberations has suggested thatnotwithstanding anonymity provisions, it is the rape defendant who is at a legal disadvantage compared with the rape complainant. The view of one juror was summed up by Rape Crisis Scotland who reflected that:

'[A] wrong decision would be more serious if found against the defendant as it would destroy a young man's future, whereas if the decision was the wrong one and found him to be innocent, the wrong committed against the woman is already in her past and therefore somehow less of a consideration'.

Assessing the merits of an argument on the basis of whether the harm is prospective of retrospective is erroneous. Doing so would fail to take into account factors including the interests of justice, public safety and public interest. Added to which, as long ag as the Helibron Report it was argued that the rape defendant's equality was with defendants in other crimes and not with the rape complainant.

CHAPTER VIII

Religious Laws and Religious Crimes: In Developing and Developed Countries

Abstract

This paper gives a survey of the writing that evaluates the connection among religion and wrongdoing. Examination on the connection among religion and wrongdoing demonstrates that specific parts of religion decreases support in crime. A survey of the writing demonstrates religion decreases interest in crime in two wide ways. To begin with, religion appears to work at a miniature level. Studies have highlighted how strict convictions are related with poise. Second, investigates have inspected the social control parts of religion. Specifically, how factors, for example, level of investment and social help from such interest diminishes crime. Moreover, discoveries propose that in spite of the fact that there has been a sizable number of studies and different interests of analysts analyzing the religion/wrongdoing nexus, the examination has not recognized which parts of religion have the most grounded effect on wrongdoing decrease.

Theoretical Underpinning of Religion and Crime

Crafted by Emile Durkheim is viewed as one of the most seasoned and most exhaustive assessments of religion in humanism. Regardless of ensuing assessments of religion in humanism, Durkheim's assessment gives a more comprehensive perspective on religion as a positive controlling power in the public eye. As per Durkheim, citizenry readily clung to center allowances of faith based expectations that either incorporated them into the structure holding the system together or managed singular practices and choices, advancing favorable to social conduct. Karl Marx is likewise truly noted for his assessment of religion which, rather than Durkheim, principally centered around the degree to which religion worked as a philosophy that been able to real cultural courses of action that propagated imbalance in the public arena.

The Sacred and Profane

Religion is made by citizenry however turns into a wonder that is otherworldly and outside to the citizenry. As indicated by Durkheim, a fundamental element of religion is the assignment of material items in the public arena as either holy (strict) or profane (non-strict) (Regnerus 2003; Ritzer and Stepnisky 2017; Sumter 1999). The assignment of bits of the material world as sacrosanct serves to build up strict assumptions/convictions in the public eye (Ritzer and Stepnisky 2017, p. 97). As individuals from strict networks are reliably aware of the differentiation between the holy and profane, so are they aware of the convictions that are addressed in the sacrosanct. This cognizant attention to the differentiation between the hallowed and profane guarantees that individuals from strict networks maintain a strategic distance from practices and choices that spoil the holy.

Survey of Literature and Religion and Self Control

This survey of the literature explores the relationship between religion, self-control, social control, and criminal behavior. This review reveals an inverse relationship between religion and criminal behavior and unmasks the potential spuriousness present in the religion-crime nexus.

Religion and Self Control

In inspecting poise, specialists have normally analyzed the manners by which mentalities, convictions, belief systems, and qualities, which are disguised, can impact the conduct of the person. Along these lines, in analyzing crime, citizenry who have joined a bunch of perspectives, convictions, philosophies, and qualities that denounce crime will be more averse to take part in such action. Religion addresses one illustration of a framework that consolidates these components.

Progressed by Gottfredson and Hirschi, discretion hypothesis expresses that people having significant degrees of poise, conceptualized as "the differential propensity of individuals to dodge criminal demonstrations whatever the conditions.

Religion and Social Control

While religion may go about as a type of poise, it can likewise be contended that specific parts of religion fill in as a type of social control also. In analyzing religion as a type of social control, social researchers ordinarily highlight the manners by which being an individual from a strict local area may apply impact over choices and practices individuals participate in. In this sense, power over practices has more to do with meeting the assumptions for the gathering and keeping an association with the gathering. It is perceived that neglecting to cling to specific practices turns into an infringement of the strict gathering's assumptions. Hence, the explanation people may avoid practices that are viewed as degenerate, is to try not to be excluded by the gathering. What's more, it has likewise been contended that cooperation in strict exercises fills in as a type of social control also. This is especially evident when these exercises are occupied with a gathering setting. Gathering support in strict exercises can be an amazing impact over conduct.

Empirical Drawbacks

Methodologically, accessible writing does not have a conceptualization of key indicator factors, especially religion. Since the last part of the 1800s, meanings of religion have been grounded in Western and Judeo-Christian calculated systems that underscore the impacts of religion on different aspects of public activity over the fundamental inceptions of religion. Besides, these conceptualizations build up religion as a characteristic and materialistic build, minimizing the heavenly elements of religion and its subordinates (Berry 2005). Thus, the related implications and significance of religion as a develop have been obliged; in this regard, religion neglects to precisely represent the large number of strict philosophies and theoretical systems that exist inside a globalized world. Inside the sociologies, this restriction blocks on exact grant into the job of religion on individual and gathering practices.

Summary

Speculation about the role of religion as an effective means of social control has a rich history with roots deeply imbedded in the functional perspective that assumes that the stability of society is maintained by teaching and reinforcing the same set of values, beliefs, and norms for everyone (Sumter 1999). This perspective is derived from Emile Durkheim, who viewed religion as a crucial and integrative mechanism for maintaining social order and fostering a set of common values and beliefs (Sumter 1999). Likewise, since the landmark study by Hirschi and Stark (1969), which questioned the effectiveness of religiosity as a social control mechanism, empirical investigations of the relationship between religiosity and crime emerged within the fields of sociology and criminology. In general, studies coalesced in revealing an inverse association between religiosity and crime; this suggests that religion helps to suppress criminal behavior (Brauer et al. 2013). Nonetheless, the religion-crime nexus remains an unsettled and controversial topic, for the evidence has not authenticated the specific mechanisms by which religiosity affects criminal behavior. As well, the research has neither rejected the possibility that the observed association between religion and crime is essentially coincidental or spurious, nor noted that the findings are inconclusive and mixed (Brauer et al. 2013; Kerley et al. 2011). Still, empirical scholarship into the religion-crime relationship persists.

CHAPTER IX

What are the Best Ways to Protect Witnesses from Retaliation in Criminal Cases?

Introduction

"At whatever point man perpetrates a wrongdoing paradise finds an observer," says Edward G. Bulwer. Witness is thusly unavoidable. Witness can have an essential part in dealing with the wrongdoer. Witness expects extra importance in ill-disposed arrangement of criminal equity where the onus of demonstrating the case lies on the indictment and the observer of arraignment gets significant in the quest for investigating reality. The situation with observer in the court is that of a companion and ally to the reason for equity. As indicated by Bentham, witnesses are the 'eyes and long stretches of equity'. It is totally fitting as the choice in the arrangement of equity that is continued in India significantly relies upon the observer and his direct. The observer has the ability to change the course of the entire case. Underlining the meaning of witness, in Swaran Singh v. Territory of Punjab, Wadhwa J. said, "A criminal case is based on the structure of proof, proof that is allowable in law. For that, witnesses are required whether it is immediate proof or fortuitous proof." It was additionally seen by him - "By giving proof identifying with the commission of an offense, he plays out a consecrated obligation of helping the court to find reality. It is a direct result of this explanation that the observer either makes a vow for the sake of God or gravely avows to talk the truth, the entire of reality and only truth. He/ she plays out an significant public obligation of helping the court in settling on the blame or in any case of the denounced for the situation. He submits himself to cross-assessment and can't decline to address inquiries on the ground the answer will implicate him" The declaration given by the observers empowers the court to choose the legitimacy of realities and conditions of the case. In this manner, the honesty of the witness' declaration turns into the foundation of the equity and subsequently the witness is committed to offer explanation having sworn to tell the truth. The assertion of witness may lead to the conviction or exoneration of denounced. The quick equity or postponement in equity conveyance additionally depends, generally, on the nature of explanation given by the observer during trail.

Perspectives to Make a Study

Encounters of witness are by and large of avoidable complaints, absence of civility, human treatment, articulation of concern, focusing and acknowledgment and broadening direction. Numerous cases concentrated in this task mirror that the observer, on a few events, was dealt with like blamed. The entire issue of witness antagonism, over which much shout is being communicated, additionally gives off an impression of being connected with the sort of treatment the observer is dispensed in the criminal equity measure. In the event that the co-activity of the observers to be acquired, the need is to comprehend the issues of witnesses. A judgment of the Supreme Court has vindicated the way that the observers experience badgering and non-thoughtful mentalities from police, arraignment and legal executive. The division Bench containing, Justice K.T. Thomas and R.P. Sethi, said that "Witnesses shake on getting summons from courts in India not on the grounds that they dread assessment or questioning but since they dread that they may not be inspected at all for a few days and on such days they would be nailed to the regions of the courts". This judgment was particularly critical from the point of witnesses. The court took genuine perspective on the intermission conceded on the unstable grounds, which put the observers in a scope of issues. The Supreme Court said that "...........it is high time that witnesses are viewed as visitors welcomed (through summons) for assisting with their declaration in arriving at legal discoveries The Supreme Court was especially searing about the way the arrangements under segment 309 of the Cr.P.C. are paraded by the courts. The segment sets out that once assessment in the court began it needs to proceed with the preliminary until all observers in participation have been analyzed. The SC completely set out that "if an observer is available in the court he should be analyzed on that day. It is currently very likely that the circumstance will improve as of now in any event, when witnesses are available suspensions are allowed to suit the comfort of the backer concerned. A significant classification of issues of witness comprises of his wastage of time and non-installment of whatever recompenses he should get for his appearance in the court. The National Police Commission focused on recompenses due to observers for appearance in Courts. The Commission noticed that the money related pay was woefully lacking and alluded to an example study did in 18 Magistrate's Courts in a single State, which uncovered that out of 96,815 observers who went to the Courts during the trial, just 6697 observers were paid some recompense, and that excessively subsequent to following a Or maybe awkward method (which unexpectedly has scarcely changed for the better anyplace). These figures connote the unimportance of the sum paid to observers for their difficulties. Aside starting here made by the Commission, these figures propose the backbreaking weight on the Magistracy, in however much every Magistrate was relied upon to look at, on an normal, around 5400 observers! Sadly, the length of the trial has not been given thus it very well might be hard to remark further on these figures; however, whatever the time frame, the circumstance couldn't at all have improved from that point forward. Numerous casualties and witnesses don't get the degree of data and uphold they need while partaking in the criminal equity measure. This disregard can frequently prompt a withdrawal of help for the arraignment, non- participation at court and disappointment with the cycle, which can result in bombed cases and hesitance by observers to reconnect in the criminal equity measure on future events. The criminal equity framework has an obligation to guarantee casualties and witnesses have a sense of security and ready to give proof. Giving proof at court is a overwhelming experience for anybody. Casualties and witnesses reserve an option to anticipate a smooth and facilitated administration from the criminal equity organizations. In an examination led abroad, it was shown that solitary 19% of witnesses felt they had been kept appropriately educated about progress for their situation. 28 percent of casualties need some type of help, while 13% say they gotten uphold. 21% of witnesses felt scared by the cycle of giving proof or by the court environment. The previous Solicitor-General, K.T.S. Tulsi said: 'legitimate observers have abandoned the criminal courts on the grounds that the police and courts regularly treat them as charged. The police regularly mentor the declaration of witnesses and stream moves them.

Witness Protection: Legal Provisions

There is no particular enactment, as exist in numerous different nations, in India only giving security to observe. Nonetheless, there are a couple of arrangements in the Indian Evidence Act, 1872. Ss. 151 and 152 that shield the observers from being asked profane, outrageous, hostile inquiries, and questions which mean to irritate or affront them. Aside from these arrangements, there is no arrangement for the security of observers in India. This reality was recognized by Supreme Court on account of NHRC versus Province of Gujarat where it said that 'no law has yet been ordered, not so much as a plan has been outlined by the Union of India or by the state government for offering insurance to the observers'. The Supreme Court said 'that there comes the requirement for ensuring the observer as opportunity has arrived when genuine and undiluted contemplations are to be offered for securing observers so extreme truth is introduced under the steady gaze of the Court and equity wins and that the preliminary isn't diminished to a joke. Authoritative measures to guarantee disallowance against altering observer, casualty or source, have become the up and coming and unavoidable need of the day.'

Conclusion

The information gathered in this investigation portray that an extensive number of witnesses shrouded in this work had higher optional or above schooling (58.6 percent). The observers with post graduation were progressively found in Maharashtra (5.9 percent) trailed by Madhya Pradesh (4.9 percent). The quantity of uninformed respondents was moreover discovered least (1.9 percent) if there should be an occurrence of Maharashtra. The rank profile of witness canvassed in this examination recommends that greater part (43.7 percent) had a place with 'General' class and 31.5 percent had a place 175 to the classification of 'Timetable Tribe' (S.T.), and just 7.1 percent of witnesses had a place with the classification of 'Timetable Caste' (S.C.) while those who had a place with the classification of other in reverse class were 17.7 percent. Larger part of the respondents in this investigation (61.7 percent) found the intermissions to be very successive. This discernment was to a great extent shared by respondents in Rajasthan (19.3 percent) trailed by Karnataka (16.7 percent). The most noteworthy number of respondents not buying in to this see came from Maharashtra (12.7 percent) while the most minimal number in this class came from Rajasthan (0.9 percent). While studying the mentalities and encounters of observers in the present investigation, 61.7 percent respondents concurred that deferments occur too much of the time and 31.8 percent were not for this see. The respondents in the previous classification essentially (43.8 percent) had a place with the 'General' classification followed by the 'Timetable Tribe' (S.T.) classification (31.1 percent). The information uncover that just about 65% observer needed to show up additional than once under the steady gaze of the court for declaration while 35.2 percent could do as such in the primary hearing as it were.

CHAPTER X

Youth Justice and Criminal Evidence Bill 1999

In a little while, the namelessness banter got back to Parliament. It was during the section of the YJCEB in 1999, where a proposed new provision, to give secrecy to assault litigants, was examined. The statement would have confined any revealing about people blamed or suspected for submitting a sexual offense that would have brought about the general population recognizing them moderate MP Mr Greenwood asked the proviso be taken to second perusing while recognizing the extremity of assessment on the matter. Some individual legal advisors accepted that the Government ought to expand secrecy arrangements others including lawful bodies, for example, the Law Society believed it to be some unacceptable move. Assessment was separated even inside individual political parties.Mr Greenwood, without extending, accepted that the interests of assault casualties were being accommodated by the Bill: he may have been alluding to proposed provisions confining the questioning of casualties in sexual offense cases. His interests lay with the comparing absence of arrangements to secure the interests of assault litigants.

Supporting his contention Mr Greenwood made reference to the thinking behind eliminating respondent secrecy in the CJA 1988: the most pervasive being that it urged casualties to approach. He alluded to various episodes that he discovered upsetting and had prompted a scrutinizing of whether 'in light of a legitimate concern for reasonableness and characteristic equity' the 'balance' ought to be reestablished. The primary occurrence concerned the self destruction of a 21 year elderly person, Mark Jackson, who hanged himself following an allegation of assault by his previous sweetheart. Regardless of his exoneration in Exeter Crown Court, the paper title texts in his old neighborhood of Wigan read 'Abandoned man, 21, assaulted ex'. The subsequent episode included the self destruction of Dennis Proudfoot. He had breathed in fumes exhaust in the vehicle following a charge of assault by his ex, purportedly through dread of the exposure it would pull in. After the man's demise his folks got correspondence from the ex conceding the allegation was false.Mr Greenwood additionally brought up that the conversation stretched out to female litigants, giving the case of a female specialist, who in 1997 was seen not as liable of disgustingly attacking a female patient. She got a decision of 'not blameworthy' of

foul attack yet was in any case exposed to public examination. Neither her profession nor her private life at any point recuperated.

Mr Greenwood contended that, while there has been a critical decrease in the quantity of assault grievances that were later 'no crimed', roughly 25% of wrongdoings were as yet recorded all things considered. The most well-known explanation refered to was that the objection was accepted to be bogus or noxious, and in 33% of such cases the complainant pulled out the charge. The idea being that in such cases it is very conceivable the litigant would have had their character unveiled and would have been exposed to every one of the implications that that caused for themselves and their families.receding conviction. The lone special cases would be the place where the character of the litigant was required to get their capture or 'is usually in light of a legitimate concern for equity'.

By contrast Mr Boateng was contrary to a representation of namelessness, summing up the thinking given by the CLRC in 1988, preceding the CJA 1988 canceled assault respondent anonymity.He recognized that '[B]alancing disgrace and post-absolution results [in an assault cases] includes contentions that are in no way, shape or form obvious' and that those proposing a revisitation of the law earlier 1988 came up short on a persuading contention. Mr Boateng upheld remarks made by Lord Falconer, during the previous considerations that alluded to one side of the overall population to realize what goes on in court. As he would see it the 'public interest' weighed vigorously in the secrecy banter however:

'[T]he present law finds some kind of harmony between the guideline of open equity, where the general population has a more extensive interest, and the vital need to guarantee that casualties of sexual offenses are urged to report such violations'.

Mr Boateng said that while some contended sexual offenses were especially grievous, the equivalent could be said for respondents of other genuine wrongdoings like homicide. To offer namelessness to assault litigants would make ready for others to contend that they likewise experience the ill effects of press and exposure. In understanding it is stated that giving assault respondents namelessness would put them at a worthwhile situation to litigants of different wrongdoings: a result that would not advance an arrangement of open and reasonable equity for all.

Mr Boateng appropriately recognized that under the Contempt of Court Act 1981, the court could arrange delay of distributions or lawful procedures for any period it considered significant. Where a court decided to retain a name from the general population during a preliminary, it likewise had the ability to deny distribution totally, in this manner on the off chance that litigant namelessness were really required, the court had the ability to authorize it

'Since secrecy for the respondent has been rejected, the idea has been hiding in the court, in pretty much every assault case, that a bogus charge may have been made under the shroud of namelessness. A man's life might be destroyed on account of that secrecy. In the event that the two players have namelessness, that idea can't hide in the foundation of the court. I recommend that that would have an effect'.

9 781638 730613